Quick Short Reference Guide

An

OVERVIEW

To

AGILE & SCRUM
METHODOLOGY

(Useful for all Developers/Programmers)

(N.GUPTA)

Table of Contents

AGILE Introduction

Agile software development is an iterative incremental development and testing throughout the software lifecycle of the project. In Agile the complete Project requirements will be broken into small incremental builds. These builds are divided into time boxed iterations and encourages rapid and flexible response to changing requirements, and with every iteration, each requirement gets tested. Testing is done immediately after development is done resulting in the early detection of the prospective defects. Once the iteration is completed the working version of the project is demonstrated to the customers. It helps in delivering the project requirements in a lesser time with better quality.

Advantages for Agile Model

- Customer satisfaction by rapid, continuous delivery of useful software.

- Team interaction with clients directly on requirement understanding

- Delivers early partial working solutions.

- Close, daily cooperation between business people, developers and testers promoting team work and cross training.

- Regular adaptation to changing circumstances.

Disadvantages for Agile Model

- It is difficult to provide required effort at the beginning of the software development life cycle, especially if it is large ones.

- There might be constantly change in the requirement

- If the customer representative is not clear about final outcome they expected then project can easily take off track.

- During development process only senior programmers are capable of taking the kind of decisions required.

- Unavailability of updated documents for reference it is difficult to transfer technology to new members.

Scrum is one of the agile frameworks structured to support complex product development work. Scrum is the most popular agile methodology. It uses for both software development and maintenance work as well. Changes can be handled in a better way in scrum as the duration of sprint is not more than four weeks and the final output is a shippable product. Unlike the traditional software methods, the end user can see the final product after each sprint and any changes can be incorporated in subsequent sprints based on business priority or environment changes. There are various roles defined in the scrum like product owner, scrum master, team etc.

In order to make the process easier, time consumption and for quick implementation we have a good handy approach in the market which plays a prominent role in making the things useful for everybody who involves in making the product release outcome.

Now a days, as per the SDLC process, we have a number of process approachable methodologies available in the market. Among all of them, the most available and significant commonly used methodology by every organization is "Agile Scrum methodology".

The main objective of the team involved in Scrum is to achieve the common business goal. The Scrum process is generally runs on the set of values which ensures the Project Success. The five main Scrum Values are as follows:

- o **Commitment**: Team should have commitment/Zeal to achieve the Goal and ensure the Successful Product to the End User
- o **Focus**: As the tasks are planned and divided for each sprint, team will focus on few items at any point of time and deliver the valuable product
- o **Respect**: While working in Agile Project, team should work together and share the failures and Success such that there will be a respect between team members which will help the organization to deliver a Worthy Product.
- o **Courage**: In Scrum, generally team will collectively take up the tasks which gives us the Courage and feel more comfortable to move on with greater challenges
- o **Openness**: In Scrum Process, team can express their views, issues faced and the suggestions to others and can ask feedback from others. This Openness will help the entire team to improve on the areas they are lagging which ultimately helps the Product quality.

SCRUM is one of the most flexible methodology of Agile. It is a kind of iterative and incremental process approach which is mostly used in the organizations where the estimation of goals changes frequently.

The most important factor to remember about the SCRUM is:

By using the SCRUM methodology, we can achieve a fast and quick sort of implementation of each piece of code within the time box of a declared sprint.

By using the SCRUM, splitting large amount of code into small pieces (sprints) of code, and making the time frame of releases of each piece of code gives a clear idea to end user.

Scrum theory is based on the three principles:

- Transparency
- Inspection
- Adaptation

Transparency

Transparency says that the people working on any process should have clear picture of all the aspects of the process. As per this principle, common standard should be followed to define the concepts and aspects of the process so that everyone in the team should have a common understanding. In other words, we can say that definition of "Done" should be same for those working on the process and those accepting the work.

Inspection

A scrum user inspects the process and determines if there is any variance that is hindering the progress of the process towards the goal. But inspection should not be too much that it affects the work. Inspection should be performed by skilled inspectors who can work hard and very careful while inspection so that it can be more beneficial.

Adaptation

If scrum inspector finds variances during inspection that are deviating the process beyond the acceptable limits and the resulting product would be unacceptable then in that case the material being processed should be adjusted. These adjustments should be made as soon as possible so that the further deviation can be stopped.

The key difference between General testing and Agile testing are as below:

General Testing	Agile Testing
Testing Phase begins once after the completion of Development Phase	Testing is a continuous activity which happens along with the Development. Even when a single module is developed.
Test Script preparation is done based on the End product and based on the requirement changes the test scripts are updated	Test Scripts preparation is done module wise and there is no changes with the scripts since there is no scope of requirement change
Test Scripts are prepared by the Testing team	Test Scripts are prepared with the combined effort of Business Analyst, Testers and End Users
QA ensure the quality of Product	All Stakeholders ensures the quality of the product
QA and Business Analyst are considered as Functional Experts	All Stakeholders are considered as Functional Experts

Agile Principles

1. Main Principle of Agile is to provide customer satisfaction for the delivery of Quality software.

2. Requirements can be changed even late in development Phase.

3. Within a shorter span (Couple of Weeks to Months) the Agile methods were able to deliver quality software

4. Developers, Testers and Business Analyst work in a coordinated way on daily basis for the successful completion of Project.

5. Equip the Agile team by building confidence and comfortable environment set up can be done.

6. One to one interaction among the team makes the Information gap fulfilled

7. Direct interaction between the Development and the testing teams makes the work done at synchronized manner

8. Providing Quality Software which is Bug Free is the end output that has to be delivered

9. Constant Pace can be maintained among the Business, Developers and testers using Agile Process.

10. Keen attention to technical excellence and proficient design upgrades the agility.

11. The Quantity and the Quality of work done is the important.

12. Requirement gathering, Design ,Develop and testing is effective with the Self Managing Agile teams

13. Regular meetings identifies the progress of work and improvement areas can be identified.

Where to use Scrum Methodology?

Scrum is one of the most flexible, malleable methodology. It is best to use scrum in an organization where goals are constantly changing and needs of customers influence the distribution of tasks in organization. So, we can say that scrum adapts itself according to the needs of the customers and business.

It implies that scrum methodology works on the actual progress of the project to plan and schedule releases. It does not depends upon the random guesses or uninformed forecast

How it Works?

- In scrum, projects are divided into clearly distinguished and well balanced modules or divided into small chunks. These chunks are called SPRINTS.

- After the completion of each sprint, team members meet and do the analysis of progress of project. And on the basis of that next step is planned.

- In this way project's direction can be readjusted depending on the actual completion of work instead of the guess work or predictions.

Note: Duration of sprints can be 1, 2 or 3 week.

- Product Owner
- Scrum Master
- Team Member

Product Owner

It is the most important role in scrum methodology. He is the person who has the highest authority of all the roles thus his responsibility is also more than all the other roles.

He is a person who communicates the vision of product to the team members who are developing that product. He explains the purpose of the product and represents the interests of customer through requirements and prioritization.

The product owner serves as the single point of contact with the stake holders and updates the team. It is the responsibility of the product owner to maintain the Product Backlog and prioritize the product backlog to provide maximum return of investment. The product owner can re-prioritize items at any time. In some cases the product owner and the customer will be the same person.

Product owner's role requires him to be available to the team every time the team needs him, shows commitment and should be actively engaged with the team. He should have good communication skills because he has to work closely with the key stakeholders so that he can communicate his ideas clearly. Simultaneously he should be able to make decisions about what features the product should have. He should have good knowledge about the market and should be able to make sound decisions.

Scrum master acts like a bridge between Product Owner and the team. His main task is to identify the obstructions or problems which teams are facing and also try to remove those obstructions, so that teams can easily achieve their sprint goals. Apart from this, his role is also to create visibility about the success of team to product owner.

The other responsibilities include planning of various meetings like sprint planning, sprint review and sprint retrospective meetings, conduct daily scrum meeting, and work with product owner to understand the system in a bigger picture and identify the business requirements.

Basically it helps team so that they work creatively and more productively.

1. Responsible for end to end flow of the Agile process.

2. Should be adhere to SDLC process throughout the process implementation

3. He is the person, who has to take the responsibility of coordinating the SCRUM teams

4. As a SCRUM master should be the SPOC for all the teams involved in the process

5. Needs to conduct the SCRUM meeting for 15 minutes everyday

6. Coordinating all the required SCRUM teams whenever any conflict raises

7. Should have Stay attached with the time and keep updating the status to Higher level

8. Development team, Infrastructure team, Testing Team, DB team, Deployment team, Production support team, Managers, Director, CAB, ECAB teams coordinated by SCRUM master

9. Keep influencing the development team for every update, and coordinate each of them if any delay is going to be happened

10. Should have to be more confident in communicating the things across the teams.

11. Should have to be committed with time and accordingly collaborates the team

12. Should be more focused and goal oriented

13. Ensuring involvement of end-user while having release meetings

14. Preparation of schedules for changes starts from DEV till to PROD

15. Needs to attend pre and post implementation review meetings

Finally, the SCRUM master is the responsible person to engage, to coordinate, and to collaborate all the teams and should be familiar with Agile SCRUM methodology.

In scrum methodology, the team works towards achieving sprint goals, which are set by Scrum Master after having discussions with team and product owner. Scrum team typically includes development team, architects, QA team, testers, and UI designers. For every sprint, the team determines how they are going to accomplish their sprint goals. This gives teams a great deal of independence in achieving their goals. But this freedom is accompanied by a responsibility to meet the goals in given time framework.

The team is cross functional and is responsible for developing and delivering the product. The team should always be in line with the product owner and should understand and aware of the scope, vision and goal of the product owner. The team usually contains 4-9 people and there is no specific roles for each team member as the team is cross functional.

Roles of QA Team

There are few roles that are assigned to the QA lead who in turn handles and transfers tasks to QA tester. The roles are described below

Roles of QA Lead

- Responsible to understand the features and Prepare test cases

- Prepare Test Cases and getting approved by the Product Owner

- Publish test Cases to QA tester & Developer Team

- Develops separate test cases to check various functionalities like Browser compatibility, user interfaces, Password functionalities and many more

Roles of QA Tester

- Performs testing of various test cases through Regression Testing, Manual Testing and other methods

- Validate Test Cases & check their functionality

For each sprint, the development team is responsible for

- To determining how it will accomplish the work to be completed

- Responsible to accurately plan to meet the goals of the sprint

- Dependencies to be properly visualized and worked over

- Daily needs to attend the Standup Call

- Daily needs to update the progress on Green Hopper

Features which make scrum popular

- Emphasis on ongoing assessment of completed work.

- Capacity for Adaptation.

- Flexibility

- Stability of practices.

Difference B/w Scrum Methodology & Extreme programming

There are very subtle differences between the Scrum Methodology & Extreme programming but are important.

- The main difference between the XP programming and scrum methodology is duration of the sprints. For scrum teams duration of sprints can be from 2 to 4 weeks whereas XP teams works in iterations which can be of duration 1 to 2 week.

- In the scrum teams changes are not allowed once the sprint meeting is completed. The set of items which are decided for particular sprint remains unchanged till the end of sprint. On the other hand XP teams are more flexible to change within their iterations. A new feature of equivalent size can be exchanged for the feature which has not been started yet.

- Extreme programming teams works in a strict priority order. Product owner determines sequence in which the features will be incorporated; And XP team follows this sequence very strictly. Whereas for Scrum Team, Product owner prioritizes the product backlog but team itself decides the sequence in which the functionalities will be incorporated or changed.

Benefits of Scrum Model

- Late prioritized changes in the requirements are adopted in the current sprint or in immediate next sprint.

- Working version of product is delivered frequently (Two weeks once) to gain customers confidence.

- Reduces the overhead and re work of the team, because it focus on prioritized User stories.

- Increases the market potential of the organization due to customer satisfaction by continues delivery of software product.

Disadvantages of Scrum Methodology

1. Makes all dysfunction visible
   - Scrum doesn't fix anything: the team has to do it
   - May feel like things are worse at the beginning

2. Bad Products will be delivered soon.

3. Doomed projects will fail faster

4. Partial adoption may be worse than none at all.

Limitations

- Scrum approach is less suitable for projects with many external dependencies.

- Scrum is not suitable for High code quality products, because in scrum ad hoc decisions are made easily. This may decrease the Code quality.

- It is not suitable for the projects holding large number of regression execution, because sprints will go in shorten timeframe in scrum.

Sprint

The team do the same set of activities repeatedly within a time box and each iteration is divided in to different sprints. The duration of iteration is not more than one month and usually more than one week. Usually the duration of sprint is fixed for the entire work. Different teams working together for the same work uses the same sprint length throughout the work. The final output of a sprint is a 'shippable product'. Only the product owner has the authority to abandon/cancel any sprints.

Daily Scrum

This is a short mandatory meeting happening on every day between the team members. It usually happens on the same location at the same time every day and the duration is not more than 15 minutes. Product owner may not be required in the daily scrum meeting, only the key members speak in this meeting. Each member will have the following updates

- What work he/she had done since yesterday

- What he/she is planning to do today

- Any obstacles/blocks to continue the work

Product Backlog

This is nothing but the deliverables or the to-do list of items in for the entire sprint. The product owner decides the priority of product backlog based on business priority and other dependencies. The highest priority items would be included in the initial sprints. There are different techniques including JIRA used to create product backlog items. The priority of items in the product backlog will change based up on Business requirements and the product owner will keep on updating the items; the product backlog is editable.

Sprint Backlog

This is a subset of product backlog. Sprint backlog is the items taken for the particular sprint and all the items would be available in a detailed manner in the sprint backlog for the sprint team. The sprint backlog is decided in the sprint planning meeting. Once the tasks are identified it will put in to the sprint backlog and there should not be any changes to this item until the sprint is completed. The members responsible for each task in the sprint also would be identified and assigned. The tasks taken in the sprint backlog is mainly time based (in an hourly basis). Scrum team will be maintaining a sprint backlog chart to update the work remaining for each team members in the particular sprint. This is usually a graphical representation and would be updated on a daily basis.

Burn Down Chart

The team uses the sprint burn down chart to track the progress of tasks of each team members in a particular sprint or release or for the product. It usually shows how much work is remaining for each team member; in the chart work remaining is plotted against vertical axis and the time period is plotted in horizontal axis. Time period can days of sprint or different sprints.

Sprint Planning Meeting

This duration of this meeting is usually 3-4 hours and maximum 8 hours for a four week sprint. The meeting happens before the sprint starts. Product owner, scrum master and the entire scrum team will be part of this meeting. The product owner along with the team will analyze the product backlog and check on the items from the product backlog. Team will analyze the items and suggest if it is feasible and commit on the product backlog at the end of the first half of the sprint planning meeting. In the second half of the meeting team will work and plan on the sprint backlog.

Sprint Review Meeting

The sprint review meeting happens after the sprint; here the team shows the working product or a demo of the work to the client. This is again a time-boxed and the maximum duration is 4 hours. The participants include the product owner, scrum master, team and other stake holders. During the sprint review meeting the overall work done during the sprint is accessed against the sprint goal identified during the sprint planning meeting.

Sprint Retrospective Meeting

This meeting is mainly intended to analyze what went wrong during the sprint and what can be done to improve on next sprints and discuss on any appreciations. The meeting is usually for 3 hours. The meeting is facilitated by the scrum master and all team members will be part of this; product owner is optional for sprint retrospective meeting.

Sprint Testing

- Sprint supports the developers in Unit Testing.

- When the test story is completed, test execution is performed by both the developers and tester together and the defects are logged in defect management tool (Quality center) which should be tracked on a daily basis. Defects should be analyzed during scrum meeting. Once the defect is resolved, it should be retested and deployed soon.

- Tester should attend all daily standup meeting to speak up.

- If there is any backlog that cannot be completed in the current sprint, tester should bring it to the next sprint.

- Automation scripts should be developed by the testers. He have to schedule automation testing with Continuous Integration (CI) system. Tester should have close communication with the team to ensure sufficient Test coverage.

- Tester should review CI automation results and send the reports to the stakeholders.

- Testers should execute the non-functional tests for approved user stories.

- Acceptance criteria for acceptance tests are defined by the testers in order to co-ordinate with the customer and product owner.

- Tester also does acceptance testing (UAT) and confirms testing completeness for the current sprint at the end of the sprint.

Scrum testing Scenario

For an agile project, the testing process should be defined up-front and performed consistently in each sprint. In some of the projects there is the full integration test for the end-to-end solution directly after the unit testing. On the projects, the team will include the regression testing which is basically serves as the integration test and more.

Unit testing helps in testing that each component is free from any bug and it should perform well. Once the unit testing is done, the following tests are to be performed in each sprint based on the needs to the solution.

- Integration testing
- System testing
- Regression test for entire solution
- Performance User Acceptance testing

In any case, if the code which is to be delivered is not working properly, the whole process of rapid delivery cycles will be executed. If the first iteration of testing is full of defects and the next iteration comes upon, the entire product will be difficult to test and there will be a pause in the project.

The testing process should be rigorous, repeatable and automated to avoid such circumstances. At the starting stage of the iterative process, we have only few requirements and few test cases. Every time when a new functionality is added, even for a small defects, we should always run the whole set of test cases.

Conclusion

Scrum Methodology is mainly useful for Fast Moving Complex Project. It ensures the Quality, Performance of the Product within scheduled time and ensures that the Product is as per the business users' requirements. It will easily adopt the changes suggested.

Clients and Other Stakeholders will review the work completed by the team on regular basis and will have an idea about the Product and can suggest the changes or modifications thus ensuring that the Product delivered will be as per the business users requirements

In Scrum, the team productivity, team commitment will be clearly visible and also there will be a healthy environment in the team which ensures the Project Success.

But, proper planning, resource allocation, well defined end target dates, monitoring the team Performance should be done properly in order to ensure the Successful Product delivery.

www.ingramcontent.com/pod-product-compliance
Lightning Source LLC
Chambersburg PA
CBHW071555080326

40690CB00056B/2047